'Ssh

JOHN ELIOT

Illustrations by
Anne Lamali

MOSAÏQUEPRESS

First published in 2014

MOSAÏQUE PRESS
Registered office:
70 Priory Road
Kenilworth, Warwickshire
CV8 1LQ

ISBN 978-1-906852-29-0

Printed and bound in the UK.

THE AUTHOR, John Eliot, was born in Leicester. He taught in the south-west of England before moving to France with his wife to write full-time. His poems appear in anthologies; *'Ssh* is his first collection of poetry. His novel *The Good Doctor* is also published in 2014.

THE ILLUSTRATOR, French artist Anne Lamali, works in a variety of techniques and media from line drawings to oils and acrylics. She mounts frequent exhibitions in the Poitou-Charentes region of France, where she lives, and has also exhibited in Paris.

The Dancer

perhaps the artist
sees herself
as a lover might
when she tears
figure from soul
stretching her upon a canvas

there to dance
ceaseless
staring in red hues
at the figure
in the exhibition
come to watch

'isn't that,' the watcher
speaks, 'that woman over there'
a head turns looking
and back
at the painting
'the model?'

coeternal
dancing with the artist

For Anne and Jill 08.10.11

The Farmer

I
The farmer wanted a good view that day.
He carefully picked out a couple of tyres.
Sturdy ones,
sound wooden platforms.
On this dais he placed his throne.
A white plastic garden chair.
Old and worn,
King of all he surveyed.

The farmer lived in the Loire.
People travelled to see what he could see.
Fields, trees, valleys.
The great river snaking reflecting the sunshine.

The farmer raised his rifle like a sceptre,
sitting in his hangar, next to his old tractor,
to peer, ready to sink,
through his neighbour's window.
But all he really wanted to see,
was eternity.
Celestial bliss.
He found it with the gunshot.

II
Knocking on the window
he waves.
Grins, but doesn't mean it.
The man is horror
Halloween cannot capture.
Haunts my nightmares,
watching him point the gun at his throat,
pull the trigger,
removing the top of his head,
like a slow motion
Tarantino movie.
No actor's performance.
His wife hears the shot,
lost opportunity realised.

The Widow

I
Strange
we heard a gunshot.
Almost at half past eight
this morning
echoing the evening
when Paul fired
blowing his brains amongst the flowers
feeding them his last thoughts.

Watching you then
Wander your empty house
Shutters drawn shielding
The cold dark winter

Holding the gun
there was only one action
lift it to the chin
repeat and repeat
like a piece of music that sticks
and will never end.

Outside the silence
blackness before dawn
hearing you tread
Walking as you will always walk
The soft tread of the dead
Painful, slow
Across field
Carrying the rifle

II
You know the way
in this blackness
Without the moon or stars
You cannot fall

Listen
the horse moves
As she hears your steps

And we all turn in our beds
Hearing the single shot thunder
Without lightning or storm or rain
We wait again for you to break the silence

III
We arrived early dawn
Mist hung over the valley
Like a spirit never leaving

The colour for a moment
Was only as God
Could capture
As if the sun
Would never rise

Hanging
Beneath the grey clouds
Lightning and then

Heavy leaden rain finally fell

Listening we could hear an echo
Of gunshot
There was no one there
To pull the trigger

The hunters lay in their beds.
Guns hung on the wall.
And the dead remained dead.

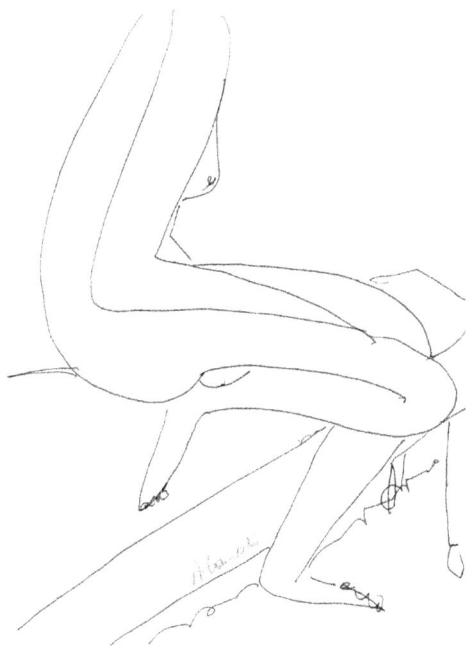

A Shadow of the Sun

running the trodden path
that no-one treads
early morning sun
still cool
promise
a thirty degree day

miles away in rhythm
thinking about the blue
I reach the end of my journey

in this deserted country two
figures are waiting
loomed out of the dark sun

for me?

a man
a woman
both watching
not standing together

they may have been smiling

I couldn't see
the man raises a hand
'all right?' he asks

the land is all wrong
they are where they shouldn't be
pain and the morning
are playing their tricks
in another place
shadows of the sun

For my son, Joe, on his thirtieth birthday

thirty years ago
(how is thirty years a long time but the memory a second?)

I held you in my arms
baby, proud Father
as a photograph

so many old photographs
where for a second
life is captured

I want to reach inside
love the moment
know again those people
whose flesh will never decay

For Joe, 25.01.11

And the black beetles sang
Without any melody
The divorce divorced and divorcee
Hating each other
So easily
Can it be that they
Knew so intimately
And the black beetles sang
Without any melody

Brussels Divorce Court 2013

The King of Thorns

for the burden is heavy
burnt by fire, a barren road
where no flowers glow
he carries his cross this

brutal sacrificial lamb
as miracles die
forgive them for
this empty tomb
dull bleak dusk
against grey sky

I never knew him
a stranger walks
on this dry earth

And paths can be
a rocky skin
From heaven where
silent yellow lightning

forks the lizard eyes
mock the man
wrapped in brown

dry thunder cracks

This is

For Kate
March/April 2012

St Cecilia

no reverence here
Japanese headphone clad
follow
forgetting worship

nearly one thousand years
St Cecilia
was buried
do they hear

her music

her tomb
lies
stone broken sunlight
face
stained glass

chapel sandstone walls
reflect silence
as in another place
cameras flash

Poem Six

The moon is full
and red
again tonight

Do you remember?

Probably not
You don't recollect a book or a film

But I think of you silly
standing barking at the door
saying
'I'm always this way
Full moon
Full moon
and tonight's it's red'

The dog is insane.

It must be a refection of the sunset
A bit like you and I caught one another

St Clémentin, France 22.09.05

Poem Ten

She rang to say
'Was that all you wanted?'

I wanted to say
She wanted to say

I love you
They both wanted to say

St Clémentin, France
October 2007

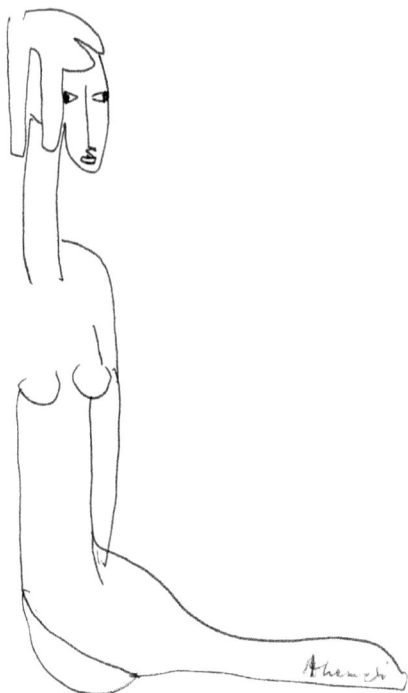

whispering poetry to bees
sung drone in return
scented blossomed air
threads of words
describing music
ommatidia reflect sunlight
wings in full flight
as barbs of the insect
terrify the poet
to creation

Journey to Barry Island

Nothing there.
Yet I heard the whistle
from Cardiff Central
twice more.
I ran
onto the platform.
Passengers
never noticed
intent on their own
journeys
my whistle and steam.
On the footplate
my Father.
Waiting for me to board
leaving behind
the past.

Changing a Fuse

how old was I
          nine
          I don't remember

too young though
 to change
     a fuse

my brother stood
          serious eyes

 part of the home stood
                    still
          no stylus grooved
          nor wireless sang
          or lamp shone

here
my dad said
you do this
and you do that

 wires
     were
cut
 a screw turned

half way up the stairs
and
half way down the stairs

I watched

not part of the scene

My sister ignored them
I never learnt

time together
Francis Cabrel
Paris
wish we could live
time again
rain beaten empty pavements
one metro home
he didn't sing
but
all night long
j t'aimerais

Poem Two

it's a Friday night
1970 I would have been
lying with
a bottle of Guinness
and a beautiful boy
now at 52
I am left with the vicar

the Beatles and the Amsterdam Hilton
how I love those words

Amsterdam Hilton

my daughter in
the room next door

she can't hear the noises of the street
(silence in sex)
that I once listened to

with her boy
she can
only hear the Beatles

Teignmouth
September 2005

26

Maggot

Such a time,
a maggot
crawled into my brain.

Can I strangle a maggot,
this myth, dream
abstract invention?

To eat upon
maggot pies and choughs.
Such stuff evaporate.

Baseless vision let me sleep.
Maggot,
let me wake.

June 2012

The Pins Don't Work

i had hoped
you'
    died
that the pins
i'
d
stuck
killed   you

the pins
don't work

pink
black
    or
blue
you

still wander
larger
    than
life
spreading
callous
cruelty

Poem One

It's a Greek afternoon
Here in dead France
So far away from
What can I say?
those who
destroy the peace
silence of
watching the vine grow

St Clémentin, France
August 2005

Sunday

snow
on the
ground

a log eyed
companion
burns

to
 my
   door
      no
       beaten
           path

January 2012

The Mother

two and a half years
more precisely
two years five months twelve days six hours and four minutes

Freddie passed away

tomorrow on the third of June at 1215pm
Freddie will be cremated
centigrade of 980 degrees it takes
to turn a baby to dust

Freddie who cried and laughed
was born from whence the angels came
being the joy of my pain
fed at my breast
loved and held
crawled and smiled
words of promise
taken by the devil
a god would not do this to me

how am I expected to watch
flesh become ash?

02.06.11

NOTRE TRÉSOR ... 21.05.13 ... Plumede .

After the Funeral

And then
quickly as the moment of death
itself
someone in the bar
at the wake
laughs

The living forget
The dead

The Rose

in the courtyard where no rose grows
a prisoner sits
empty eyes stare

in a moment they will come
return him to his cell
to sit and lie
for twenty three hours alone
eat, wash, defecate

stare at a TV screen
a child's face the prisoner sees
in his cell where no rose grows
in his cell where no child goes

May 2011

Breakfast in Belgium

Break Fast in Belgium
shortestday
through pane
wheels spin rain

735am
Piped carols ♫
Hark The Herald Angels

poised 'tween
plate & mouth
mirabile dictu
the mystery

of how
Jesus liked his bacon

A motel in Belgium, Vilvoorde
December 2011

Christmas

wake up blackness
chill tells me

Christmas

too early to wish you

Merry

turning to hold your warmth
loveliest gift of all

December 2011

Two Magi and a Swan

They travelled so far
guided by light
to see this sight
baby held
by Mother tight

old King reverence bent knee
another I couldn't see
hidden
for the artist
there

amongst them stood a Prince
pr'aps Son of the King
gazing not in adoration
but at
Me

telling the world
I am here

and from below
His robes
a Swan's neck
curved

After Antwerp Cathedral
December 2011

New Year

'It's nearly midnight!'
a drunken man shouts

and people feign excitement
5 4 3 2 1

another year

Shall we countdown to our deaths?

A man I can't abide
approaches
extending a hand
woman
with florid face
broken veins
like vines
pouts for a kiss

December 2011

The girls at school
tell stories of Christmas.
The parties.
Boyfriends.
Presents and fancy houses.

For me there has always been nothing.
Barely fed.
Barely clothed.
Sexually abused.

Merry Christmas to you all.
I am the girl with a house,
but no home.

After the Festival

My rest I shall take.
Amongst the apples
ready to pluck
the leaves to fall.

Poetry to write.
For branches
are lines bare
against the autumn sky.

Juice the verse
inside the peel
to drip comme les mots tears?
onto my page.

08.09.12

Bach

Sombre joy
Sitting obsession
in an airless room
half closed shutters

Somewhere far off
a harpsichord plays
Bach
Drops a fourth
here and there
But who am I to care?

Clouds move grey
on this October day
I might tread out
by a river
into trees beyond
where ghosts roam

Far away from a chateau
a figure at a window
stands watching
He doesn't see
listening as notes
are picked one by one

Carefully now
as though
Life mattered
when it is
Death that bears ignorance
like Birth

What does any of it mean?
Music echoes
drifting along
passageways
In and out of
empty rooms
I search for the player
There is nothing
Only the sound

I am alone
I am alone
No one is here for me
on this chilly
October day
holding onto figures
disappearing

Poetry Day 2012

Ssh
Listen
Sound of rain
Failing light
Train across rails
Steam effort
Far echoes
Silence
Ssh

1970-2014